**Joanna Phillipson**
A kitten (a tabby I could call Tabitha), three hamsters, a pony, lots of sweets (chocolate, please), and a candle making set. That's it!

**Natalie Davie**
I'd like a dog — a dalmatian — and a rabbit, a guinea pig and another hamster. I already have a hamster called Fudge, and I'd call my new one Smartie.
I'd also like a gadget dog — you stroke its head and it moves like a real dog. But it'd be really good if people would stop killing wild animals for their tusks and coats.

**Helen Walker**
A ticket for a Boyzone concert.
Sean the Sheep back-pack and one of those big hairy puppets that looks as though it walks.
And to stop all forest fires.

**Iona McIntosh**
A dolphin! You can adopt a dolphin which has a transmitter on it, so the Dolphin and Killer Whale Society can tell where it is and what it is doing.
I would also like fishermen to stop blowing up coral reefs to get at fish. That would be a good present, too.

**Zoe Dias**
A new tennis racquet. Mine is a bit old and scratched and it isn't big enough! If possible, I'd like some tennis balls and a tennis racquet case, too.
I'd also like to save the rain forests and get lots of bamboo for the pandas to eat.

£5.15

D1243407

# what's in?

## Your Bunty Annual 1999

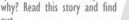

Printed and Published in Great Britain by D.C.Thomson & Co., LTD., 185 Fleet Street, London, EC4A 2HS. © D.C.Thomson & Co., LTD.,1998
ISBN 0-85116-663-6

Soon —

HOW ABOUT THIS PERFUME FOR YOUR MUM?

GROSS! IF SHE WORE THAT, WE'D ALL HAVE TO SPEND CHRISTMAS DAY WITH PEGS ON OUR NOSES!

OOPS! LOOKS LIKE IT'S TIME TO MOVE ON, LAURA. I DON'T THINK THE SALESLADY LIKED YOUR OPINION OF THAT PERFUME.

HEY, LOOK! IT'S GRIM GERTIE. SHE'S BUYING A TIE!

WONDER WHO IT'S FOR? HER BROTHER, PROBABLY.

OR HER SECRET BOYFRIEND! HA! HA! WHAT A THOUGHT!

HELLO, LAURA! BECKY!

OH! ER — HELLO, MISS GRIMSTYLE!

YIKES! THINK SHE HEARD US?

SHE COULDN'T HAVE. SHE SMILED AT US!

HI THERE, YOU TWO!

HI, CLAIRE. HI, NIKKI! YOU DOING LAST MINUTE CHRISTMAS SHOPPING, TOO?

YUP! BUT WE'RE JUST GOING FOR SOME FRIES AND A COKE. WANT TO JOIN US?

So — THIS SURE BEATS HOMEWORK!

ANYTHING BEATS HOMEWORK, CLAIRE!

TRUE! HEY — WHAT'S THAT NOISE? I CAN HEAR 'JINGLE BELLS'.

IT'S THESE MUSICAL SOCKS. I GOT THEM FOR MY DAD!

JINGLE BELLS

HA! HA! HA!

TRUST YOU, NIKKI!

WHAT A NAFF PRESENT. I THINK I'LL GET SOME FOR MY DAD!

OW!

DID YOU SEE THAT MAN PUSHING INTO THE LIFT? HE DIDN'T HAVE TO SHOVE ME LIKE THAT! TALK ABOUT RUDE!

OH, NO! MY PURSE! IT'S GONE, BECKY!

OH, LAURA. THAT MAN MUST'VE BEEN A PICKPOCKET!

THEY'LL NEVER CATCH HIM. THAT WAS ALL MY CHRISTMAS MONEY, BECKY. HOW AM I GOING TO BUY ANY PRESENTS NOW?

The girls found a policeman —

THE SUSPECT IS DESCRIBED AS ABOUT FIVE NINE, UNSHAVEN, IN HIS THIRTIES . . .

WE'LL KEEP AN EYE OUT FOR HIM, GIRLS.

POOR LAURA, I . . . HEY! LOOK!

8

9

# WHAT'S cookin'?

# EASTER YUMMIES

A fabby feast of spring goodies!

## LEMON FAIRY CAKES
### (Makes 16)

**Light as air!**

### INGREDIENTS
100g **self-raising flour, sifted**
100g **margarine**
100g **caster sugar**
2 **eggs**
grated rind of 1 lemon
100g **icing sugar**
yellow food colour
sugar flowers and hundreds and thousands
paper cases

### METHOD
1. Place the flour, margarine, caster sugar, eggs and lemon rind in a large bowl and beat until the mixture is light and fluffy.
2. Place two teaspoons of mixture into each paper case and place in a pre-heated oven at 160°C, 325°F, Gas Mark 6 for 20 minutes, until well risen and firm to touch. Allow to cool on a wire rack.
3. Mix the icing sugar with approx. five teaspoons of water and one drop of yellow food colour.
4. Spread icing on top of cakes and have fun decorating with the little sugar flowers — or any other decorations you can think of.

## CHOCOLATE NESTS
### (Makes 18)

**'Egg'stra special!**

### INGREDIENTS
100g **dark chocolate, chopped**
75g **butter**
2 tbsp **golden syrup**
100g **cornflakes**
paper cases
small chocolate sugar coated eggs

### METHOD
1. Place a large bowl over a pan of simmering water.
2. Add the chopped chocolate, butter and golden syrup. Melt gently.
3. Remove bowl from heat and add the cornflakes. Stir well to coat cornflakes evenly.
4. Spoon into paper cases and place three eggs on each nest.
5. Leave to set for at least two hours, if you can wait that long!

## EASTER BISCUITS

**Crumbs, they're crunchy!**

### INGREDIENTS
100g **butter, softened**
75g **caster sugar**
1 egg **separated**
1 teaspoon **mixed spice**
200g **plain flour**
75g **raisins**
grated rind of 1 lemon
1 tbsp **milk**
caster sugar for sprinkling

### METHOD
1. Beat together butter and sugar until light and add the egg.
2. Sift in the flour and mixed spice.
3. Add the raisins, lemon rind and milk.
4. Remove from bowl and knead lightly to bring mixture together.
5. Roll out onto a surface dusted with flour. Cut into rounds with a large biscuit cutter.
6. Place on baking trays and cook at 200°C, 400°F, Gas Mark 6 for 15 minutes. Dust with caster sugar.

Always ask an adult's permission before using kitchen equipment.

10

# COMPUTER CRAZY

AMY was in town with her mates —

ANT AND I ARE GOING SKATING THIS EVENING.

SO ARE MARK AND I.

I'LL TRY AND TALK KEV INTO IT. IT'D BE NICE FOR US ALL TO GO.

ALL EXCEPT ME. THEY MEAN.

I WISH I HAD A BOYFRIEND, TOO. I FEEL LIKE THE ODD ONE OUT ALL THE TIME. AMY ON HER OWN, THAT'S ME!

LOOK AT THIS CARD I'VE GOT FOR KEV.

I HARDLY SEE THE GANG THESE DAYS — THEY'RE NEARLY ALWAYS OUT WITH THEIR BOYFRIENDS.

WELL, MUST GO. I'VE GOT TO PHONE KEV.

I THINK I'LL HEAD FOR HOME.

AND ME.

I MAY AS WELL GO, TOO. I WAS GONNA DO SOME CHRISTMAS SHOPPING, BUT I'M NOT IN THE MOOD NOW.

Next day, Amy went back to the shops —

HI, AMY.

WHAT? OH! HI, GARY.

I REMEMBER BEFORE EMMA MET ANT SHE WAS CRAZY ON GARY. I SUPPOSE HE IS QUITE NICE.

11

12

YEAH, GARY HOLMES. WE'RE GOING OUT NOW.

OH!

IT'S TRUE. I SAW HIM YESTERDAY AND I'M SEEING HIM TONIGHT, TOO.

ANT WOULD LOOK COOL IN THAT TOP.

MMMM, SO WOULD GARY.

IT'S TERRIFIC NOW THAT I'VE GOT SOMEONE TO TALK ABOUT, TOO!

KEV'S STARS SAY HE'S GOING ON A JOURNEY. WHAT'S GARY'S STAR SIGN, AMY?

I DON'T KNOW. WE'VE NEVER TALKED ABOUT BIRTHDAYS.

As the days passed —

IN FACT, WE NEVER TALK ABOUT ANYTHING APART FROM COMPUTER GAMES!

YE-ES! GOT IT!

IT'S HOW WE SPEND ALL OUR TIME. I LIKE HAVING A BOYFRIEND, BUT SOMETIMES I GET BORED.

FANCY COMING OUT FOR A WALK NOW?

NOT JUST YET.

HUH! HE MEANS NOT AT ALL!

● WHEN Gemma Wale told us that her ambition was to be a magician, we knew exactly what to do. We said "Abracadabra!", waved our magic wand and . . . nothing happened! So what did we do next? We took Gemma to meet Richard, the chairman of The Young Magicians Club, and Karen, a young magician, who were willing to show Gemma a few tricks of the trade.

**2** This floating ball trick is known as The Silver Moon. How *does* Karen do it?

**1** Ready to go. Gemma is given a magic cloak. Wonder if it has special powers?

ABRAC

Gemma learns how to stick spikes through her mum's arm. Nice! Er — shouldn't you be looking scared, Mum?

**3**

**4** Now chair levitation. Gemma was the one who found *this* scary.

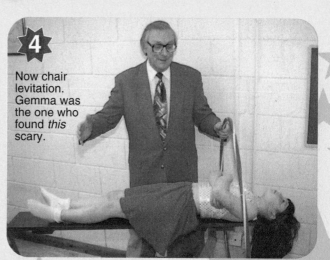

A new outfit — and a new skill. Gemma has fun with a diabolo.

**5**

**6** Then plate spinning. Oooh! Careful, Gemma. You've got to concentrate.

**7** Wow! Look at that footwork! She's getting better . . .

# CADABRA!

**8** . . . . and *better*! How's that for a finish? Five plates, all spinning at the same time.

Gemma certainly had a "magic" day out. Anyone interested in The Young Magicians Club can contact them at The Hertfordshire Business Centre, Alexander Road, London Colney, Herts AL2 1JG

17

# Carly's Crowd!

**H**I, guys!
I guess you know that the fourth Thursday in November is Thanksgiving Day in America, right? It's cool.

Now, last Thanksgiving, me and the crowd wanted to do something real special.

"But Thanksgiving is *always* special," Mom said when I told her. "I mean, you get to have turkey and cranberry sauce for Thanksgiving dinner."

"Sure we do," I said. But I could tell Mom didn't *really* understand. So I spoke to the gang.

"I have to be home for Thanksgiving because we have about a zillion of our family visiting with us," Marie Gomez explained. "They're coming on a special holiday flight from Mexico City."

"That's cool," Lori said. "It means you'll have a special day, anyway, right?"

"Right," Marie said. "But what are *you* guys going to do?"

"We're having a meal at home, like always," Lori said.

"And we'll be having a family meal," Sammy said. "Like always."

"I have this great idea," I said. "What if *we* make a Thanksgiving meal for all our families? We could do it at my place and Mom can go round to Lori's while we cook."

Marie shook her head.

"Good luck, guys. I figure you're going to need it."

★　　　★　　　★

But, when I spoke with Mom, she wouldn't go along with the plan.

"You mean you don't trust us?" I accused her.

"It's not whether I *trust* you or not, honey," Mom said. "I'm sure you and the guys can handle this just fine, but I have to be around, okay? But I promise I won't lift a finger — short of a complete disaster, which we *know* won't happen."

You know what, guys, I wish Mom hadn't said that last bit.

"I never realised how much planning and stuff you need to do just for one meal," I said to Lori and Sammy the day before Thanksgiving.

"But we did everything in the end," Lori said.

"Isn't our turkey the biggest you ever saw?" Sammy said.

"I figure it's not as big as the one Marie Gomez' mom has to feed her zillions of family," I said.

Now that it was nearly time, we were all excited. Sammy and Lori stayed over, and we had a great time telling spooky stories all night.

★　　　★　　　★

Only problem was, the next morning we slept late.

And when Mom *did* wake us, it was with bad news. And I mean *bad*.

"You know what, guys," Mom said, "we forgot something yesterday."

"We did *everything,*" I insisted.

Mom shook her head.

"Everything except take the turkey out of the freezer. You guys forgot. And it didn't do much good for you to have a grown-up around, because *I* forgot

too. It's still frozen solid!"

"So we take out the turkey and we put it in the microwave oven to thaw, huh?" I grinned. "No problem!"

Sammy shook her head.

"This *is* a problem, Carly. Even if we could thaw it out in time, that turkey is not going to fit into a microwave any smaller than the one belonging to the Jolly Green Giant!"

It was then I heard the phone.

"I'm calling to see how you guys are getting on with preparing your meal, on account of how I've got nothing to do right now." It was Marie Gomez — and did she sound bored?

"I thought you'd be helping your mom," I said.

"Well, for one thing, the turkey's already in the oven. And, for another thing, it shouldn't be — because our guests aren't going to make it. The flight's been cancelled! I tell you, I'm going to be eating turkey until Christmas."

I told Marie about our own disaster. Only, halfway through my telling her, she said "hold it" and the phone went dead. I had only just put our phone back on the rest when it rang again.

"Hi," Marie said. "You guys fancy Thanksgiving with the Gomez family?"

And so, guys, in the end we had a real different Thanksgiving Day after all. Me and Mom, and Lori and her folks, and Sammy and her folks, all eating with Marie's family.

It worked out so well, guess we really did have something to give thanks about, huh?

# Fear of the Future

FIONA NELSON and her mates were on a trip to the seaside —

I CAN'T WAIT TO TRY OUT MY INSTANT CAMERA! COME ON, GIRLS, SMILE!

THERE! BRILLIANT!

YEAH! BUT COME ON, FIONA. LET'S HEAD FOR THE FUN FAIR ON THE PIER.

WAIT A MINUTE. HOW ABOUT TRYING THIS FORTUNE TELLER?

NO WAY! IT'S JUST A CON. I BET SHE CAN'T REALLY SEE INTO THE FUTURE.

JODIE'S RIGHT. BUT YOU GO IF YOU LIKE. YOU CAN CATCH US UP AT THE FAIR.

ROMANY
Rita Lee
ADVICE
HEALTH
BUSINE
BE
F
IS

20

21

A few days later —

GUESS WHAT! I'VE GOT A BOYFRIEND! HE'S CALLED KEITH AND HE'S A BIT OLDER THAN US, BUT HE'S GORGEOUS.

LUCKY YOU, JEN. WHERE DID YOU MEET HIM?

HIS FAMILY'S JUST MOVED IN OPPOSITE ME. HE'S COMING TO COLLECT ME FROM SCHOOL LATER!

YOU MEAN HE'S GOT A CAR?

NO! A MOTOR BIKE.

BRILL!

OH, NO! JEN SHOULDN'T GO ON THE BACK OF A BIKE. SHE COULD BE HURT! THAT COULD BE THE ACCIDENT THE FORTUNE TELLER SAW. JEN WILL HATE ME IF I RUIN HER ROMANCE, BUT I'VE GOT TO DO SOMETHING!

So —

MY COUSIN DAVE WILL COME IN HANDY.

SCHOOL CHARITY WANTED COLLECTORS

DAVE! REMEMBER I LOOKED AFTER YOUR GOLDFISH WHILE YOU WERE ON HOLIDAY? WELL, NOW I NEED A FAVOUR . . .

At four o'clock —

JEN! CAN I HAVE A WORD?

SURE, DAVE.

23

Next day, at school —

SOMEONE SPOILED THINGS FOR ME WITH KEITH. IF I EVER FIND OUT WHO IT WAS, I'LL KILL HER!

OO-ER! I ACTED FOR THE BEST, BUT JEN WOULD NEVER BELIEVE THAT.

A few days later —

WELL PLAYED, JODIE. I'D LIKE YOU TO JOIN THE SCHOOL HOCKEY TEAM.

CONGRATULATIONS!

YEAH! WELL DONE!

WE'VE AN AWAY MATCH AGAINST FAIRFAX ON SATURDAY.

OH, NO! THEY PLAY ROUGH! JODIE COULD GET THUMPED BY A HOCKEY STICK — OR THERE MIGHT BE AN ACCIDENT OR SOMETHING. I'VE GOT TO STOP HER BEING IN THE TEAM, JUST IN CASE THIS IS THE DISASTER THE FORTUNE TELLER SAW.

So —

OW! MY ANKLE!

OH, I'M REALLY SORRY, JODIE. IT WAS AN ACCIDENT.

IT'S SWELLING UP A BIT. IT'S NOT SERIOUS, JODIE, BUT I'M AFRAID YOU WON'T BE FIT TO PLAY ON SATURDAY. I'LL HAVE TO CHOOSE SOMEONE ELSE FOR THE TEAM.

OH, FIONA! I'VE LOST MY PLACE AND IT'S ALL YOUR FAULT!

SHE'LL THANK ME IF THERE'S AN ACCIDENT AND SHE'S NOT INVOLVED.

24

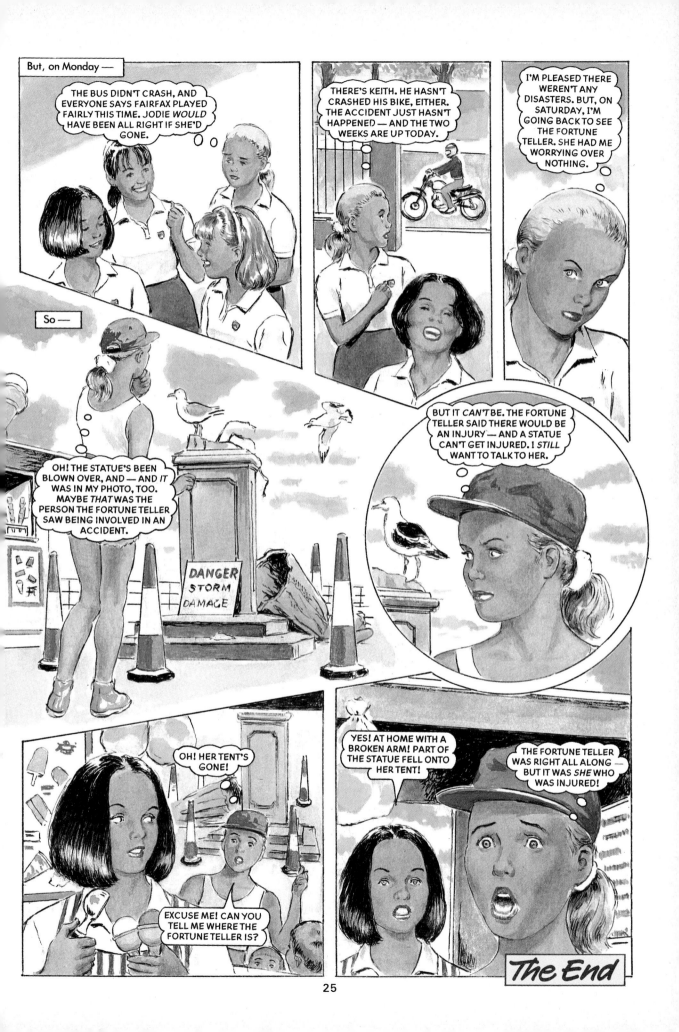

# Do Not

## Jodi
from
Swindon
shows us a few of
her very special things
— after she's finished
reading her favourite
magazine, that is.

When she's not reading, Jodi's crazy about sport. Here she shows off her swimming certificates.

Ice skating is another of her top hobbies . . .
. . . and roller skating, too. Jodi wears her merit badge with pride.

Jodi's certainly not scared. She and some friends have formed their own ice-hockey team (gulp). Here she is with her brother, David. Jodi's the fierce-looking one on the right!

26

# Disturb!

Even examining insects for a school project doesn't bother Jodi. This girl is scared of *nothing*!

Mind you, she's always got her pet, Ben, to protect her. He's been in Jodi's family longer than *she* has, because he was bought before she was born.

Here's Jodi's favourite outfit! Nice 'n' spicy!

After all that sport, Jodi loves to relax with her cuddly toys. Her favourite is the duck — called Gary.

Jodi loves painting her nails. The redder the better. (But *not* with her spicy outfit.)

**Thanks for showing us round, Jodi.**

# LOVE THY NEIGHBOUR

WENDY and her parents had come back to their old house after living abroad for two years.

RENTING THE HOUSE TO ANOTHER FAMILY WHILE WE WERE AWAY WAS A GOOD IDEA. THEY'VE LOOKED AFTER EVERYTHING WELL.

IT'S GREAT TO COME BACK TO THIS PLACE. I CAN'T WAIT TO SEE ALL MY OLD FRIENDS.

AND AT LEAST WE ALREADY KNOW THE NEIGHBOURS.

OH, NO! I'D FORGOTTEN ABOUT PAUL THE PAIN NEXT DOOR. I DON'T WANT TO SEE *HIM*. I'VE HATED HIM EVER SINCE HE BOUGHT ME A PLASTIC SPIDER FOR MY TENTH BIRTHDAY.

Later —

D'YOU THINK THERE'S ANY CHANCE THE SMITHS HAVE MOVED, MUM? IT'LL BE THE ANSWER TO ALL MY PRAYERS IF I NEVER HAVE TO SET EYES ON PAINFUL PAUL, THE TOTAL PRAT, EVER AGAIN!

OH, WENDY! I . . .

PAUL! TEA'S READY.

COMING, MUM!

OH, NO! HE MUST HAVE HEARD WHAT YOU SAID, WENDY.

OOPS!

MIND YOU, WHY SHOULD I WORRY? I DON'T CARE *WHAT* PAUL THINKS OF ME!

28

Soon Wendy returned to her old school —

WELCOME BACK, WENDY.

GREAT TO SEE YOU. YOU LOOK DIFFERENT.

SO DO YOU TWO. WE'VE ALL GROWN UP A BIT IN THE LAST TWO YEARS, I SUPPOSE.

SURE HAVE. KATE AND I ARE WELL INTO BOYS NOW.

SUE'S GOT A *HUGE* CRUSH ON PAUL SMITH! HAVEN'T YOU, SUE?

PAUL? THEY'VE *GOT* TO BE JOKING!

DON'T LOOK, BUT THERE HE IS NOW! OHHH! HE'S *SOOO* GOOD-LOOKING!

P-PAUL? *WOW!* HE'S DROP-DEAD GORGEOUS! WHAT ON EARTH MUST HE THINK OF ME, SAYING THOSE AWFUL THINGS IN THE GARDEN.

BUT WHY SHOULD I CARE? HE MAY BE GOOD-LOOKING, BUT HE'S STILL THE BOY WHO CRASHED MY TRIKE AND USED UP ALL MY PAINT WHEN WE WERE LITTLE. HE'S *STILL* A PAIN!

After school —

I'VE INVITED THE BOWENS ROUND THIS EVENING. THEY WANT TO HEAR ALL ABOUT OUR TIME OVERSEAS.

I BET PAUL WON'T COME. NOT AFTER WHAT I SAID ABOUT HIM.

But he did —

HELLO, WENDY.

HELLO, PAUL.

THIS IS THE PITS! I DON'T KNOW WHAT TO SAY TO HIM.

29

But, an hour later —

YOU KNOW, I THOUGHT TONIGHT WAS GONNA BE AWFUL, WENDY, BUT I'VE ENJOYED SPEAKING TO YOU.

ME TOO! NOW, ARE YOU GOING TO GO ROUND TO YOUR PLACE AND GET ME THAT CD YOU PROMISED?

SURE, I . . . OOPS!

OH, YOU CLUMSY FOOL! THAT'S JUST *TYPICAL* OF YOU, PAUL BOWEN. YOU'VE RUINED MY BEST JEANS!

HUH! IT WAS AN ACCIDENT — BUT I DON'T SUPPOSE *YOU'D* BELIEVE THAT!

NO WAY! NOT WITH *YOUR* RECORD. YOU'VE CAUSED ME NOTHING BUT TROUBLE SINCE WE WERE TINY.

By next morning Wendy had calmed down, and —

THERE'S PAUL! HE DOESN'T LOOK ANNOYED NOW, EITHER.

ER — HI, PAUL.

HI, WENDY. I'LL GET YOU TO SCHOOL. OKAY?

Soon —

I'M CALLING IN HERE FOR A MAG, PAUL. D'YOU WANT TO WAIT?

SURE, BUT THAT SHOP'S ALWAYS PACKED. LEAVE YOUR BAG WITH ME WHILE YOU GO IN.

But, when Wendy came out —

HE'S WITH A MATE, AND THEY'RE LAUGHING — JUST LIKE HE USED TO WHEN HE'D PLAYED A PRACTICAL JOKE.

OKAY, WHAT ARE YOU UP TO? YOU'VE PUT SOMETHING IN MY BAG, HAVEN'T YOU, JUST LIKE YOU DID WHEN WE WERE LITTLE? I SAW YOU LAUGHING.

OH, FOR GOODNESS SAKE, WENDY. WE WERE LAUGHING AT A JOKE. I HAVEN'T *TOUCHED* YOUR BAG.

30

# Bunty - a girl like you

# Make Your Own... Snowstorm!

Snowstorms are great fun. Just give them a shake and you have your very own snowstorm — indoors! Follow the instructions to make a great gift or keepsake for yourself.

## You Will Need:

Miniature Christmas cake decorations, e.g. a Santa, Christmas tree, robin, reindeer or snowman.
Strong, waterproof adhesive.
A small glass jar with a screw-on lid, such as an empty hair-gel jar or honey pot.
Two dessertspoonfuls of desiccated coconut OR a tube of glitter.

## To Make:

1. Wash the jar and let it dry thoroughly.

2. Coat the bases of the Christmas cake decorations with the adhesive and stick them to the bottom of the inside of the jar. Holding each ornament in place with a pair of tweezers till the adhesive sticks will help to position them better. Allow plenty of time for the adhesive to stick.

3. Add the desiccated coconut or glitter.

4. Fill the jar with vinegar to the top OR fill with water, if you are using glitter.

5. Coat the inside of the rim of the lid with adhesive, so that when screwed on, it sticks firmly in place and the jar is watertight.

*Now you have your very own snowstorm. A gentle shake is all that's required to make your snow scene come alive!*

# GABBY'S OWN GOAL

**T**HERE was only one thing Gabby Palmer hated more than her kid brother, Ben — and that was football.

GIVE ME BACK MY BALL, GABS.

YOU LITTLE MONSTER — YOU SPILT MY DRINK!

JUST WAIT TILL I GET YOU!

AND I WAS HAVING SUCH A NICE DAYDREAM ABOUT ZAC SIMPSON, TOO.

IF ONLY I COULD FIND A WAY TO GET TO KNOW HIM.

A few days later —

I'VE JUST BEEN ACCEPTED BY THE JUNIOR FOOTBALL CLUB, MUM!

THAT'S GREAT NEWS, BEN.

HUH! NOW THERE'LL BE EVEN *MORE* FOOTBALLS FLYING AROUND!

36

So —

THIS WASN'T QUITE WHAT I HAD IN MIND, BUT AT LEAST I GET TO WATCH ZAC TRAIN.

IT'S GREAT TO BE HERE.

MY SISTER, LIZ, WOULD AGREE WITH THAT. SHE USUALLY COMES ON A SATURDAY.

Afterwards —

YOU'RE A GOOD SPORT. OUR LIZ WOULD LIKE YOU. FANCY SEEING A MOVIE ON FRIDAY NIGHT, GABBY?

YES! I'VE GOT A DATE WITH ZAC!

SURE! THERE'S A GREAT FILM ABOUT FOOTBALL ON AT THE EMPIRE.

On Friday —

NOW TO SHOW OFF TO ZAC.

NOW SHOWING

I SEE ROVERS HAVE SIGNED RODNEY LEWIS. HE'S SOME STRIKER, ISN'T HE?

ER, YEAH. I SUPPOSE HE IS.

After the football film —

THAT WAS A BRILLIANT FILM, WASN'T IT, ZAC?

YOU'RE SO LIKE LIZ. YOU'RE BOTH FOOTBALL CRAZY!

HERE, TAKE THIS, BEN AND GET LOST FOR A WHILE.

I'M OUTTA HERE!

COME AND SIT DOWN.

ER, BETTER NOT, GABBY. YOU SEE, I THINK IT'S TIME WE SPLIT UP.

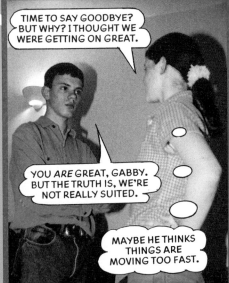

TIME TO SAY GOODBYE? BUT WHY? I THOUGHT WE WERE GETTING ON GREAT.

YOU *ARE* GREAT, GABBY. BUT THE TRUTH IS, WE'RE NOT REALLY SUITED.

MAYBE HE THINKS THINGS ARE MOVING TOO FAST.

BUT WE CAN STILL BE FRIENDS — MEET AT THE FOOTBALL CLUB.

FRIENDS, YES. FOOTBALL CLUB, NO. I'VE ONLY BEEN HELPING OUT WHILE MY SISTER WAS AWAY.

ZAC, *PLEASE* DON'T! WE CAN WORK THINGS OUT!

NO. YOU *LOVE* FOOTBALL AND I *HATE* IT. I CARE ABOUT YOU TOO MUCH TO ASK YOU TO GIVE IT UP FOR ME. GOODBYE, GABBY.

Too late, Gabby realised that, through her deception, she had scored an own goal!

SO ZAC'S *SISTER* IS THE FOOTBALL FAN! IF ONLY I'D JUST BEEN MYSELF . . .

THE END

# TOP DOGS

Aww! Aren't they cute? Thanks to all the Bunty readers for sending in these fab photos of their four-legged friends.

● Lucky MILOU lives in the Seychelles with Karen. He loves going for rides in cars, boats and wheelbarrows!

● Aoife has written a poem about her pup, BAILEY.

*I have a dog — his name is Bailey,*
*I feed him well and walk him daily.*
*We have such fun — he loves to play,*
*I love my dog in every way.*

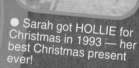

● Sarah got HOLLIE for Christmas in 1993 — her best Christmas present ever!

● BEN and TESSA are best buddies. Tessa loves girlie things like dressing up, while Ben is much more laid back, says their owner, Carly.

● Labrador LUCY is the colour of chocolate and just as sweet. Her owner, Zoe, says she's the best dog in the world!

● Orla is nuts about CRACKERS, her spaniel. Crackers is four and loved very, very much!

41

# BEN

**K**ATIE was floating on her back in a warm, blue sea. Waves lapped at her cheeks, chin and forehead. Then suddenly, she woke up to find Ben licking her face.

"Morning, Ben," she smiled.

Her dog nuzzled his face into her shoulder. He loved Katie and came to wake her every morning.

"It's the first day of the holidays today, boy. Let's go for a walk up Redmond Hill."

Katie's mum packed a picnic for them, then off they set.

\* \* \* \*

The view from the top of the hill was spectacular — you could see for miles. Katie felt on top of the world as she and Ben sat and ate their picnic.

Afterwards, Katie lay back and soaked up the sun. Soon, she had nodded off, with Ben snoring happily beside her.

Suddenly, a splash of cold water hit her on the nose. The sunny day had gone. Now the sky was heavy and the first drops of rain had started to fall. It was time to make for home, and fast.

As they began their descent, there was a clap of thunder and jagged lightning streaked across the sky. The rain now fell faster, bouncing off the ground and starting to form small rivulets which made their way down the hill.

Halfway down, there was a large, overhanging rock and Katie decided to take shelter under it until the worst was over. She and Ben huddled together for warmth.

Suddenly, Katie heard an extra-loud rumbling noise that she knew wasn't thunder.

"It's a landslide, Ben!" she shrieked. "We must get away!"

Ben was by her side as she ran from beneath the rock and looked back. A sea of boulders and mud was rushing towards them. She was aware of Ben trying to push her out of the way of the danger, when she lost her footing and screamed. Then there was blackness.

Katie came round to feel Ben licking her face. At first she thought it was morning and she was in bed. But then she remembered the wall of rocks and mud coming towards her.

Now she could see the sky was blue. The storm was over, but how long ago? How long had she been unconscious?

Ben was fussing, pleased she was awake, and Katie realised he had been keeping her warm. She tried to sit up, but her head hurt.

Ben started to run away for about a metre and then return to her. He did this several times, whining.

"You're telling me to get home, aren't you, boy?"

Katie held on to his mud-slicked coat and pulled herself up slowly. Her head was swimming, but she knew she had to try. She held on to Ben all the time, but they were very slow.

Just then, Katie heard someone calling.

"It's Mum and Dad, Ben! They've come to find us!" she shouted.

In a few moments her parents were there, fussing over her worriedly. Katie explained what had happened.

"Ben saved me," she said, and turned to pat him. But Ben had disappeared.

"Where did he go, Mum? Did you see him?" Katie sounded frantic.

"Knowing him, we'll probably find he's waiting for us when we get home," said Mum. "But first we must get you to the hospital."

\* \* \* \*

The doctor ordered Katie to rest for a day or two. But she could not settle because Ben was not home.

"He saved my life, Mum," she wept. "He'd never leave me, ever. I was hurt and he knew it. He helped me."

"Maybe he's in shock," said Dad. "That's why he ran off. Let's go back to Redmond Hill and look for him."

They were soon there, trudging through the drying mud and fallen stones towards the large broken rock where Katie had sheltered.

"Thank goodness Ben was with you to help," Mum was saying.

But just then Dad stopped and pointed down towards the fallen rocks. His face was pale.

"Ben *couldn't* have helped you down," he stammered.

Katie shivered when she saw what Dad was looking at. She couldn't understand it, but somehow, Ben had loved her so much that nothing, absolutely nothing, would stop him from protecting her.

"Thank you, Ben," she sobbed, staring at the ground.

And there, lying peacefully, was Ben, half trapped beneath the rocks that had killed him in the landslide.

**THE END**

# WHO'S NEXT DOOR?

JODIE MILLER lived in a small village. One evening —

THIS CONVICT HAS ESCAPED FROM MOORSTON PRISON. ANYONE SEEING HIM IS ADVISED NOT TO APPROACH.

OO-ER! MOORSTON PRISON'S NOT FAR FROM HERE.

JODIE! COME HERE!

WHAT IS IT, MUM?

SOMEONE'S MOVED IN NEXT DOOR. LOOK! THERE ARE LIGHTS AT THE WINDOWS.

GREAT! I HOPE THEY'VE A DAUGHTER MY AGE.

44

45

THERE'S PROBABLY A DANGEROUS CRIMINAL LIVING NEXT DOOR TO US, AND NOBODY CARES BUT ME!

RUBBISH! YOU'VE BEEN WATCHING TOO MANY DETECTIVE PROGRAMMES.

IF YOU WATCHED THE NEWS INSTEAD, YOU'D KNOW THE HUNT FOR THE ESCAPED PRISONER HAS MOVED TO FRANCE NOW. HE'S LEFT THE COUNTRY.

SO THE POLICE THINK. BUT THEY COULD BE WRONG!

Next day —

IT'S NO USE WATCHING DURING DAYLIGHT. OUR NEIGHBOUR NEVER GOES OUT. I'LL HAVE TO WATCH AT NIGHT.

At last —

A CAR'S PULLING UP OUTSIDE!

HE'S GOING OUT! I CAN'T SEE HIM CLEARLY FROM HERE. I NEED TO BE DOWN IN THE BUSHES TO POSITIVELY IDENTIFY HIM.

So, the next evening —

MUM AND DAD THINK I'M ROUND AT A FRIEND'S. I CAN STAY HERE ALL EVENING AND THEY'LL NEVER KNOW.

47

49

# flower power!

GEMMA FOSTER loves helping out at a friend's flower shop. Luckily, she doesn't have to get up at 4.00 am to buy the flowers at the market!

Gemma makes sure the fresh flowers look their best inside AND outside the shop.

A dried flower arrangement gets the finishing touch.

Gemma enjoys wrapping the flowers.

A bouquet ready for delivery. Someone's going to be lucky!

Serving customers is always fun.

A clean sweep — the shop must be kept spotless.

There are floral decorations for every occasion.

All the plants are well watered.

Phew! Time for a breather. It's a bloomin' hard job — but great fun!

# SUMMER SPECIALS
## Party food for indoors or out!

## SWEETCORN SALAD
(Serves 10)
*INGREDIENTS:*
*2 x 390g cans of sweetcorn, drained*
*3 tomatoes*
*1 red pepper*
*8 spring onions*
*4 tbsp mayonnaise*
*2 tsp wholegrain mustard*
*Black pepper*

**METHOD**
**1.** Chop the tomatoes and red pepper into small dice.
**2.** Wash the spring onions and slice thinly.
**3.** Mix the prepared vegetables and the drained sweetcorn with the mayonnaise and wholegrain mustard. Season with black pepper.

## BARBECUE CHICKEN DRUMSTICKS

(Serves 10)
*INGREDIENTS:*
*10 chicken drumsticks*
*2 tbsp clear honey*
*1 tbsp Worcestershire sauce*
*2 tbsp orange juice*
*1 tbsp tomato puree*
*1 tbsp soy sauce*
*Black pepper*

**METHOD**
**1.** Mix all the sauce ingredients together and pour over the chicken which has been placed in a shallow, oven proof dish.
**2.** Leave to marinate for 30 minutes, covered with cling film.
**3.** Pre-heat oven to 190°C, 375°F, Gas Mark 5 and remove cling film.
**4.** Place chicken in the oven for 35 minutes until golden dark brown and thoroughly cooked. Serve hot or cold.

## CHERRY MERINGUE KNICKERBOCKER GLORY
(Serves 2)
*INGREDIENTS:*
*1 can of red cherries in syrup*
*4 small meringue shells*
*4 scoops of vanilla ice-cream*
*Spray cream*
*Hundreds and thousands to decorate*

**METHOD**
**1.** Take two tall glasses and put 2 tbsp of red cherry mixture in the base of each.
**2.** Place one meringue shell and one scoop of ice-cream on top of fruit.
**3.** Place another 2 tbsp of red cherry mixture on top of the ice-cream.
**4.** Finish with the second meringue shell, another scoop of ice-cream and 1 tbsp of cherry mixture.
**5.** Top with lots of cream and decorate with hundreds and thousands. Eat immediately!

*Always ask an adult's permission before using kitchen equipment.*

55

Next day, in town —

I LOVE DOING SURVEYS. IT'S LOADS BETTER THAN BEING IN THE CLASSROOM.

OH, OF ALL THE LUCK! LOOKS LIKE WE'VE GOT SARAH SUPERVISING US!

WORKING HARD, AMY? HERE, I'VE GOT YOU A DRINK.

OH! ER — THANKS, SARAH.

THAT'S NICE OF HER. TROUBLE IS, SHE HASN'T GOT ONE FOR ANYBODY ELSE, SO I'M BEING SINGLED OUT AGAIN. I THINK I'LL TRY TO KEEP OUT OF HER WAY FROM NOW ON.

Next day, after registration —

I HEAR YOU'VE BEEN CHOSEN FOR YOUR JUNIOR HOUSE HOCKEY TEAM, AMY? WELL DONE! YOU SEEM TO BE SETTLING IN WELL.

HOCKEY TEAM? ME? BUT I'M RUBBISH AT HOCKEY!

WE KNOW WHY YOU'VE BEEN PICKED, DON'T WE? SARAH'S GAMES CAPTAIN IN YOUR HOUSE. WELL, IT'S NOT FAIR. WENDY PLAYS BETTER THAN YOU.

I KNOW. LOOK, I'LL TELL SARAH I WON'T PLAY.

THEY'RE BEGINNING TO RESENT ME, BUT IT'S NOT MY FAULT!

At break —

I NEED SOMEONE TO HELP ME FOR A FEW MINUTES. AH, YOU'LL DO, AMY.

HEAR THAT? 'YOU'LL DO, AMY.' SURPRISE, SURPRISE!

YEAH — PREFECT'S PET!

COUNT THOSE PAPERS PLEASE, AMY, AND PUT THEM IN ALPHABETICAL ORDER.

WHY HAS SHE BOTHERED ASKING FOR HELP? THAT'S NOT A BIG JOB.

56

After break —

IT'S FREEZING OUT THERE!

SEE, I GOT YOU IN OUT OF THE COLD, DIDN'T I, AMY?

OH, SHE'S MAKING THINGS EVEN WORSE! I WISH SHE WOULDN'T TRY TO BE NICE. I'D RATHER HAVE MY FRIENDS BACK.

CREEP!

PREFECT'S PET!

I WISH I'D NEVER COME TO THIS SCHOOL! THIS IS AWFUL!

But, next morning —

LOOK, AMY, I'D LIKE TO BE FRIENDS WITH YOU, REALLY. IT'S JUST BEEN HARD, YOU KNOW?

THANKS, LOUISE. I DON'T WANT SARAH TO SINGLE ME OUT LIKE SHE DOES, EITHER. I REALLY DON'T UNDERSTAND WHAT'S GOING ON.

Soon the girls were fooling about —

THERE, TAKE THAT!

WATCH IT, YOU! HA! HA!

OH, IT'S GOOD TO BE MATES AGAIN.

STOP THAT STUPID BEHAVIOUR THIS MINUTE! BOTH OF YOU! OR YOU'LL BOTH GET A DETENTION!

HEY! SHE TOLD ME OFF!

WELL, IT SURE MAKES A CHANGE, SHOUTING AT HER PRECIOUS AMY!

But, later that day —

AMY TOLD ME YOU HURT HER THIS MORNING. COME AND SEE ME LATER, LOUISE, FOR YOUR PUNISHMENT.

EH? WHAT'S SARAH TALKING ABOUT? I NEVER SAID ANYTHING TO HER! SHE'S MAKING IT UP!

# Sammi's Stars

ONE evening, at Sammi Farrow's house —

WHO WANTS A DRINK?

OH, BRILLIANT, SAMMI!

DO YOU WANT ONE, EMMA?

EH? OH — SORRY, SAMMI. I WAS JUST READING MY HOROSCOPE.

SO WHAT'S GOING TO HAPPEN TO YOU THIS WEEK, EMMA?

I'M GOING TO WIN A LOT OF MONEY! IF ONLY!

YOU'RE A SCORPIO, AREN'T YOU, SAMMI? LET'S SEE WHAT IT SAYS FOR YOU.

YOU NEEDN'T BOTHER — IT'S ALL RUBBISH ANYWAY.

HEY, LISTEN TO THIS! 'SATURDAY WILL BE YOUR LUCKY DAY. AN OLDER BOY WILL BRING ROMANCE.'

THAT'LL BE RIGHT! THIS TIME NEXT WEEK I STILL WON'T HAVE A BOYFRIEND — YOU WAIT AND SEE!

60

61

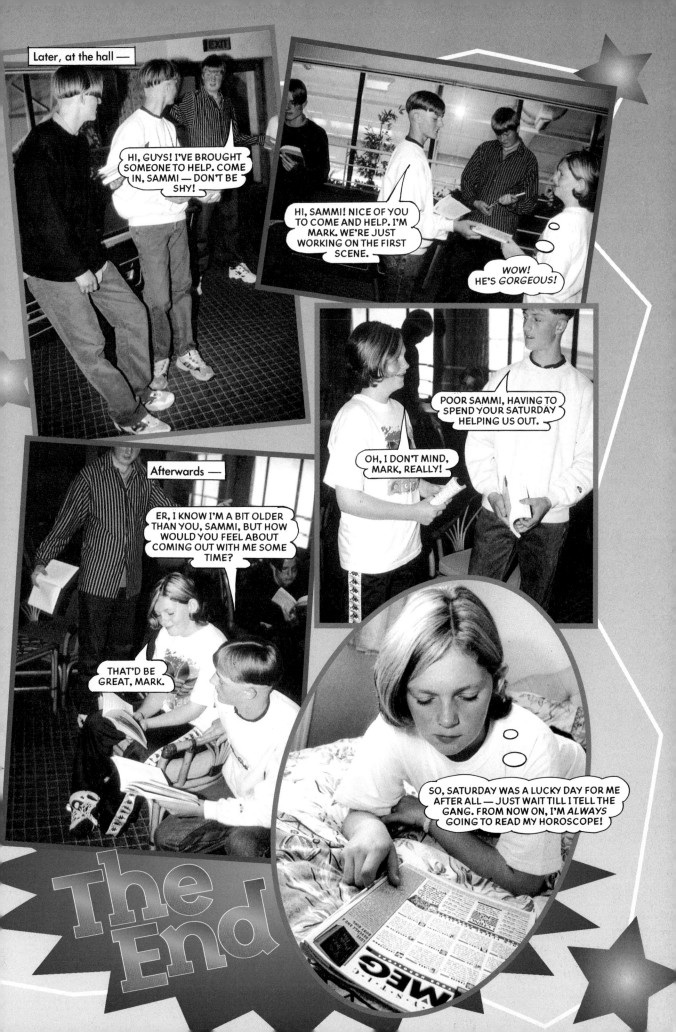

65

**Rebecca Ormerod** lets us sneak a peek at all her favourite things!

# Do Not Disturb!

Special souvenirs from a very special holiday — at Disney World!

Cinderella or Snow White? Who do you think Rebecca will look like in her favourite dress?

Time for a tune! Rebecca takes a seat at her keyboard and prepares to play!

More music! Rebecca picks out her fave CD — by Take That! Remember them? (She also loves Spice Girls!)

Rebecca collects unusual pencils! They're gathered together in her special holder.

And there's more! Just look at all these keyrings!

Aw! Time to snuggle up with some cute 'n' cuddly friends!

## TELLY WATCH

**Find the following words hidden up, down, backwards, forwards and diagonally in this tough TV wordsearch:**

BYKER GROVE, BROOKSIDE, BLIND DATE, BAYWATCH, BART, BAZZ, BIANCA, BECKY, CASUALTY, CLUELESS, CALIFORNIA DREAMS, CHANDLER, DAN, DARLENE, ER, EASTENDERS, FRIENDS, FRESH PRINCE OF BEL AIR, GRANT, GLADIATORS,

GOOSEBUMPS, HOMER, HOLLYOAKS, JOEY, JAMBO, JUDE, JACKIE,

KURT, LISA, MONICA, MADGE, MARK, NEIGHBOURS, PHOEBE, PAT,

PHIL, PEGGY, ROSS, RUTH, ROY, RACHEL, RICKY, ROSEANNE, SISTER SISTER, SABRINA THE TEENAGE WITCH, SWEET VALLEY HIGH, SAVED BY THE BELL, SESAME STREET, THE SIMPSONS, TOP OF THE POPS, TELETUBBIES.

```
A S E N G B A Y W A T C H E N E L R A D J T
B F R E A D Y E J S N O S P M I S E H T L E
R O Y I C A D K U R T D I Q U V W T I K R L
C T P G I N T E E R T S E M A S E S M N A E
D A A H N S M A E R D A I N R O F I L A C T
L I T B O K R A M O G E J S Y R P S O Q H U
L D H O M E R K A S U R P E X R E R Y S E B
E A F U P A B L D S V H O T A O G E K P L B
B L H R Q S F E G E I J K V B S G T C M P I
E G I S I T S M E L W L L Y E E Y S I U R E
H C T I W E G A N E E T E H T A N I R B A S
T A B E R N N T P U X F Z S C N Z S U E S T
Y S E D A D U D Q L Y Z M K D N E H T S D G
B U C I V E G B S C A G N A F E G C H O F H
D A K S B R W A R B T O P O F T H E P O P S
E L Y K X S H R S Z A H O Y U V Y W E G T I
V T R O S S E T A D D N I L B I A N C A N O
A Y L O Z R Y N T B C R E L D N A H C J A B
S M F R E S H P R I N C E O F B E L A I R M
J O N B C I E I K C A J P H X Z A K L N G A
K S W E E T V A L L E Y H I G H B E E D U J
```

# ISSION!
## to these terrific telly puzzles?

## YIKES!

Who's in trouble here? Name the character and the soap in which he appears.

## MUM'S THE WORD!

Write the answers to these questions in the grid below and a CORONATION STREET mum will appear reading down in the shaded area.

1. Phil and Grant's EastEnders mum. (5)
2. She's mum to DJ, Darlene and Becky on Channel Four. (8)
3. She calls her son William in Brookside but his dad calls him Billy. (6)
4. Rosie and Sophie are her Coronation Street daughters. (5)

## ALL CHANGE!

Change BART into LISA in just four easy steps, changing just one letter at a time. Easy!

BART
1. ——
2. ——
3. ——
4. ——
LISA

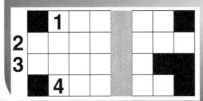

## WORDS! WORDS!

How many words of three letters or more can you make from the letters in 'EASTENDERS'?
Scores
15-20 FAIR
21-25 GOOD
26+ EXCELLENT

## ODD ONE OUT

Who's the odd one out in these three groups?

(1)
PO
TINKY
WINKY
LAA-LAA
KOOKY
DIPSY

(2)
MONICA
PHOEBE
CHANGER
ROSS
JOEY

(3)
DARLENE
HOMER
BART
LISA
MAGGIE

69

# Autumn Apple Surprise

**Two fab fruity recipes for you to try!**

## APPLE AND CINNAMON CAKE

**Ingredients:**
200g margarine
200g soft brown sugar/muscovado sugar
3 eggs
125g walnuts, chopped
200g self-raising flour
2 tsp baking powder
350g cooking apples, peeled, cored and grated
2 tsp cinnamon

**Topping:**
25g soft brown/muscovado sugar
50g walnuts, chopped

**Method:**
1. Pre-heat the oven to 180°C, 305°F, Gas Mark 4.
2. Grease and line a 9 inch (23 cm) deep round cake tin.
3. Beat all the ingredients together, except for the cooking apples, until well blended. This will take about 2 minutes.
4. Spoon half the mixture into the tin, smooth with a knife, then sprinkle with the grated apple.
5. Spoon over the remaining cake mixture and level the surface.
6. Sprinkle with the topping of nuts and sugar, and bake for 1¼ hours until the cake is golden brown and well risen. Leave to cool on a wire rack.
   **Serve with lots of vanilla ice-cream.**

## APPLE SCONES

**Ingredients:**
**Half** a cooking apple, peeled, cored and chopped
100g self-raising flour
½ **tsp** baking powder
50g margarine
50g caster sugar
50ml milk
25g demerara sugar
pinch of salt

**Method:**
1. Pre-heat oven to 400°F, 200°C, Gas Mark 6.
2. Sieve flour, salt and baking powder.
3. Rub in margarine till mixture resembles fine breadcrumbs. Add sugar and apple.
4. Mix to a soft dough with the milk.
5. Roll out on a floured surface, form into a round shape, and mark into wedges.
6. Place on a baking tray and brush with milk. Next, sprinkle with demerara sugar and bake for 20 minutes.

**Always ask an adult's permission before using kitchen equipment.**

70

# The Four Marys

THE FOUR MARYS, Cotter, Field, Radleigh and Simpson, were friends in the third form at St Elmo's School for Girls. One day, in early December —

ONLY ANOTHER TWENTY-THREE DAYS UNTIL CHRISTMAS, VERONICA! I CAN'T WAIT!

QUIET, MABEL! WE'RE TRYING TO WORK.

MABEL CAN'T HELP IT, MISS CREEF! HER DAD'S BUYING HER A PORTABLE TV AND A VIDEO RECORDER FOR CHRISTMAS! SHE'S SO EXCITED!

CHRISTMAS IS NOT JUST ABOUT RECEIVING PRESENTS, MABEL. IT'S ABOUT GIVING, TOO. NOW GET ON WITH YOUR WORK.

After school —

WHAT ARE YOU GETTING YOUR MUM THIS YEAR?

I DON'T KNOW YET.

HEY — LOOK! THERE'S A CIRCUS SETTING UP ON THE COMMON!

DO YOU THINK MRS MITCHELL WILL LET US GO?

I DON'T KNOW IF I WANT TO. I DON'T LIKE CIRCUSES IF THEY HAVE WILD ANIMALS. I THINK IT'S CRUEL.

SATURDAY'S PERFORMANCE IS CANCELLED? BUT *WHY*?

MY FATHER'S UNCLE HAS DIED IN ITALY. MY PARENTS AND SOME OF OUR OLDER RELATIVES HAVE TO GO HOME FOR THE FUNERAL.

**CIRCUS**

SATURDAY'S PERFORMANCE CANCELLED

DOGS
CLOWNS
HORSES

WE CAN'T PERFORM THE SHOW WITHOUT THEM — SO WE'LL HAVE TO CANCEL.

OH, WHAT A SHAME. THE CHILDREN'S HOME WILL MISS OUT, TOO.

WE CAN'T LET THAT HAPPEN. THERE MUST BE A WAY TO SAVE SATURDAY'S SHOW.

HOW ABOUT IF WE HELPED OUT?

YEAH! WE'LL ASK OUR HEADMISTRESS, MRS MITCHELL AND LET YOU KNOW AS SOON AS POSSIBLE. DON'T DO ANYTHING UNTIL YOU HEAR FROM US.

Back at school, the Marys explained —

I THINK IT'S AN EXCELLENT IDEA, GIRLS. I'M SURE SOME OF THE STAFF WILL JOIN IN, TOO.

*WHAT?* WELL, *I* CERTAINLY WON'T!

OH, MISS CREEF, CHRISTMAS IS ABOUT *GIVING*. AND THIS IS A *CHARITY* SHOW.

HMPH!

The girls started rehearsing immediately —

YOUR GAMES TEACHER WILL BE IN THE ACROBAT TROUPE, BUT WE'RE STILL ONE SHORT.

I'LL DO IT!

But —

AARGH!

ER — I DON'T THINK ACROBATICS IS QUITE YOUR THING, MABEL.

FALLING OVER IS, THOUGH. SHE CAN BE A CLOWN!

AND FIELD CAN JOIN THE ACROBATS. SHE'S AN EXCELLENT GYMNAST.

SIMPY AND VERONICA CAN BE CLOWNS, TOO. NOW, WHO'S GOOD WITH HORSES?

RADDY IS.

WHAT CAN I DO?

WELL, THERE'S GINO'S ACT.

FIRE-EATING? NO WAY!

IT'S ALL RIGHT. GINO'S NOT GOING TO THE FUNERAL, BUT MY AUNT IS. COULD YOU DO HER JOB — CARRYING ON THE FLAMING TORCHES . . . AND STANDING STILL WHILE GINO THROWS KNIVES AT YOU?

COTTY WILL NEVER DO THAT! SHE'S TOO SCARED!

But —

WOW! SHE NEVER EVEN FLINCHED! SHE'S BRAVER THAN I THOUGHT.

THAT'S WHAT THEY THINK! I'VE TAKEN MY CONTACT LENSES OUT, SO I CAN'T SEE ANYTHING!

What happens if you eat Christmas decorations? You get tinselitis!

Where do spies shop? The snoopermarket!

What do you get from nervous cows? Milkshakes!

Who has friends for lunch? A cannibal!

What do witches eat for breakfast? Snap, cackle and pop!

What do thieves eat? Beef-burglars!

HA-HA-HAPPY CHRISTMAS!

Heaps of jokes to make you smile!

What's white and goes up? A silly snowflake!

How do you make a Swiss roll? Push him off an Alp!

What do police drive underwater? Squid cars!

What would you call a bald koala? Fred bear!

What planes do dragons fly? Spitfires!

What is a mermaid? A deep-she fish!

What's big, bright and stupid? A fool moon!

What's the best day to buy chips? Fry-day!

76

# THE COMP

THE pupils of Redvale Comp always entered a float in Redvale's Torchlit Winter Carnival. There was a price for the best float, so it had to be special.

WE'VE GOT TO WIN THIS YEAR — OR AT LEAST BEAT THE HIGH SCHOOL, AND THAT SNOOTY GIRLS' SCHOOL, ST ANGELA'S!

YEAH!

WE NEED A GOOD THEME FOR A FLOAT — BUT *WHAT*?

HOW ABOUT HENRY THE EIGHTH — THEN WE CAN CHOP OFF A FEW GIRLS' HEADS!

GROSS, HODGE!

I KNOW! HOW ABOUT A PIRATE SHIP?

Laura drew up a design and, a few days later —

THE COMMITTEE HAS CHOSEN 9B'S IDEA, SUBMITTED BY LAURA BRADY!

WE DID IT! WE'LL BE IN THE CARNIVAL!

BUT I MUST REMIND EVERYONE THAT OUR FLOAT THEME MUST BE A SECRET!

TOO RIGHT! WE'RE NOT HAVING THOSE OTHER SCHOOLS NICK OUR IDEA!

The art department was to build the float —

EXCELLENT, LAURA! BUT WHY THE PARROT?

PIRATES *ALWAYS* HAVE PARROTS!

Slowly, the float took shape —

IT'S LOOKING GOOD, LAURA!

SURE IS, ROZ!

I CAN'T WAIT TO START ON THE PARROT!

SSSSH, HAYLEY! THERE'S TWO ST ANGELA'S GIRLS OVER THERE — I KNOW THEM FROM HOCKEY!

*I KNEW* IT! THEY WERE TRYING TO LISTEN IN!

WHAT A NERVE!

Next day —

WE'D BETTER STOP. IT'S GETTING DARK, AND THAT LIGHT KEEPS FLICKERING.

Then —

STUPID KIDS — WANTING TO BE IN A PATHETIC CARNIVAL!

IT'S THOSE CREEPS, PIPPA AND MORAG! LOCK UP, QUICK. IF THEY SEE OUR FLOAT, THEY'LL TELL EVERYONE — JUST OUT OF SPITE!

79

# GREEN scene

## NEW YEAR NEW YOU?

**Want to be as green as possible next year? We'll tell you how!**

**1** Collect stamps for charity and take paper and bottles to recycling points.

**2** Never waste water or electricity. Turn off taps as you brush your teeth and don't leave lights on in empty rooms.

**3** Don't be a litter lout. Litter looks awful, takes ages to biodegrade and can be harmful to wildlife.

**4** Support your favourite charity. Help to raise money through sponsored events or buying goods which bear their name.

**5** Keep an area in your school or garden specially for wildlife. Plant flowers to attract butterflies and bees.

**6** Put a plant in your room. Certain plants can act as filters, reducing the pollution caused by chemical cleaners and air fresheners.

**7** Out shopping, re-use your carrier bags.

**8** Put up a bird table in your school or garden. It'll help to feed wild birds and you can watch them, too!

**9** Want to get fit? Try rambling or bird-watching with friends. You'll be out in the fresh air, enjoying the countryside.

**10** Buying cards or wrapping paper? Use recycled products wherever possible.

## brrr!

**When it's cold, how does wildlife cope? We've got all the info!**

- Whales and seals keep cosy with a thick, warming layer of blubber.
- Hamsters hide food away in lots of secret locations so they've a 'store' for the winter months.
- Certain animals, like stoats, change colour from brown to white so they're camouflaged in winter snow.
- Reindeer scrape away at snow to reveal lichen underneath — an essential snack.
- Bactrian camels from Asia have cosy coats to keep them snug in the cool desert.
- Lucky penguins never feel the cold. They have thick oily feathers to protect them.

## don't Pollute Polar bears

The North Pole — home of the majestic polar bear — may be thousands of miles away, but the effect of pollution and global warming can still be felt there.

Pollutants such as pesticides and oil can contaminate the Arctic environment by evaporating from polluted soil, and condensing in the cold Arctic air, or travelling there more directly through rivers and streams.

This doesn't immediately affect the health of animals as large as polar bears — huge creatures, which grow to a height of 1½ metres and a length of three metres — but will eventually take its toll as their food sources — such as smaller seals — become affected.

Global warming is also an important issue as the world's climbing climate is currently melting away the polar bear's habitat.

# TREE-MENDOUS

**TALLEST —**
In Australia a eucalyptus tree grew to 152m!

**SMALLEST —**
Dwarf willows, found in the Scottish mountains, grow to just 2½cm!

**DEEPEST —**
A wild fig in South Africa has roots that reach down 120m!

**BROADEST —**
Calcutta Botanic Gardens has an Indian fig with a canopy that covers around three acres!

## survival

**If** you had to live through winter surrounded by cold water, how do you think you'd get on? Keeping warm and water-proof is a difficult job for ducks, who have to pay close attention to feather care. First, they clean their feathers by splashing, rolling, thrashing their wings and throwing water over themselves. Next, they give themselves a good shake, then start preening — placing the feathers back in place and covering them with oil from the preen gland above their tail to keep themselves waterproof!

## water ways

**BIRDS** need water even in the coldest of weather, both for drinking and cleaning their feathers, so try to make sure there's always a fresh supply of water in your garden — free from ice and placed where cats can't reach it.

What can *you* do to help? Walk or use public transport whenever possible (and encourage your friends and family to do so as well); try not to use pesticides in your garden; around the house, use products which are environmentally friendly.

## DID YOU KNOW...

. . . when reindeer walk, their hooves make a crunching, crackling noise?
. . . they usually live for 12-15 years?
. . . reindeer are excellent swimmers?
. . . they're the only species of deer where the females have antlers?
. . . they are often domesticated and used to provide transport for people living in the Arctic?

## WHO'S HIBERNATING

In the wild in winter, all kinds of animals curl up against the cold. Like who? Check our list and find out!
● Bears burrow down in river banks, caves and cosy, dry holes for the winter months.
● Snakes sometimes snuggle up together in groups!
● Bats hibernate hanging upside down with their wings wrapped round themselves to keep cosy!
● Hedgehogs have a long five-month hibernation spell, curled up under bramble bushes and covered with grass and leaves. Cosy!

## FACT FILE
### POLAR BEAR

**HABITAT:** Edge of the ice sheet around the North Pole.
**APPEARANCE:** Dark skin to absorb heat from the sunlight. White fur, which acts as camouflage and insulation against the cold.
**FOOD:** Seals, birds.
**SPECIAL FEATURES:** Superb sense of smell Ability to eat up to 40kg of food in one go! Thick layer of blubber under skin provides insulation against the cold.

# Girls Talking

# Christmas Past

I'D LOVE YOU TO HAVE HAD THIS PLACE WHEN I WAS LITTLE, MUM. IT'S LIKE SANTA'S GROTTO — I'D HAVE BEEN IN HEAVEN!

WELL, THAT YOUNG LADY THERE SEEMS TO LIKE IT . . .

MAXINE'S parents had just taken over a toy shop. It was nearly Christmas and Maxine was helping them in her school holidays.

. . . SHE'S ALWAYS COMING IN. KEEP IN EYE ON HER, WILL YOU?

YEAH, I'VE SEEN HER BEFORE . . . HEY, YOU DON'T THINK SHE'S A THIEF, DO YOU?

I WONDER WHO SHE'S WITH?

But —

SHE WAS HERE TWO SECONDS AGO, BUT SHE'S JUST DISAPPEARED INTO THIN AIR.

— EXCEPT, OF COURSE, PEOPLE DON'T DISAPPEAR. I'VE JUST LOST HER IN AMONGST THE OTHER SHOPPERS.

Later —

SHE'S IN AGAIN. SHE DOESN'T LOOK VERY HAPPY, DOES SHE?

MUM'S RIGHT, SHE NEVER LOOKS HAPPY AND SHE ALWAYS LOOKS QUITE SCARED BY SOMETHING.

AAH!

IT'S AS IF SHE'S NEVER SEEN THINGS LIKE THESE BEFORE.

WHO IS SHE? AND WHAT'S SHE DOING OUT ALONE? I MUST FIND OUT.

The next day —

THERE SHE IS! I HAVE TO TALK TO HER THIS TIME.

But —

DRAT! MISSED HER AGAIN!

IT REALLY IS AS THOUGH SHE JUST VANISHES — BUT I KNOW THAT'S DAFT.

That evening —

...ANTED TO TALK TO HER — I'M ...ORRIED ABOUT HER. IT'S ...EARLY CHRISTMAS AND ...RYONE SHOULD BE HAPPY, ...UT I'VE *NEVER* SEEN HER SMILE.

CAN I COME TO THE WHOLESALER WITH YOU, DAD?

YEAH, LOVE, I DON'T SEE WHY NOT.

LETS GET SOME MORE HI-TECH STUFF — THAT'S WHAT EVERYONE'S AFTER THIS YEAR.

YEAH, THESE DAYS EVEN LITTLE GIRLS DON'T SEEM TO WANT DOLLS.

THE END

# PENNY'S PLACE

HEY, LOOK! THE CHESTERFORD COACH COMPANY IS RUNNING SPECIAL TRIPS TO THE LAKELAND CENTRE!

PENNY JORDAN's parents ran Penny's Place café in Chesterford. One day, in December —

THAT PLACE IS SO COOL! IT'S GOT ALL THE BEST SHOPS.

AND IT'S ONLY TWO HOURS ON THE COACH FROM HERE!

YEAH! LET'S GO! WE COULD GET SOME CHRISTMAS SHOPPING!

YOU'LL HAVE TO COUNT ME OUT, GUYS. I'VE NO DOSH FOR THE FARE, LET ALONE TO SPEND.

The evening before the trip —

SHOULDN'T YOU BE IN BED, ARLENE? YOU'VE AN EARLY START AND A LONG DAY TOMORROW.

AW, MUM! I'M JUST WATCHING THE END OF THIS MOVIE.

91

And, next morning —

OH, NO! I FORGOT TO SET MY ALARM! THE COACH LEAVES IN TWENTY MINUTES!

A little later, at the bus station —

WHERE'S ARLENE? THE COACH IS ABOUT TO LEAVE!

IT IS LEAVING, PENNY!

Then —

SORRY I'M LATE!

YOU IDIOT, ARLENE! YOU'VE MADE US MISS THE BUS!

IT'S OKAY, PENNY. THERE'S ANOTHER ONE IN AN HOUR AND A HALF. WE CAN STILL GO.

And, later —

WELL, HERE WE GO — BETTER LATE THAN NEVER.

I'VE SAID I'M SORRY!

IT'S OKAY, ARLENE. IT COULD HAPPEN TO ANYONE. LET'S JUST FORGET IT.

After half an hour —

HEY, WHAT'S HAPPENING? THE COACH WASN'T SCHEDULED TO STOP ANYWHERE, SO WHY ARE WE SLOWING DOWN?

Then —

SORRY, LADIES AND GENTLEMEN. WE HAVE A FAULT WITH THE BRAKES. THIS COACH CAN'T GO ANY FURTHER.

WHAT?

OH, NO!

93

95

# CHRISTMAS CRACKERS!

## WHAT'S cookin'?

## CHOCOLATE SLICE

### INGREDIENTS
100g butter
250g dark chocolate, broken into pieces
3 tbsp golden syrup
350g digestive biscuits
100g raisins

### METHOD
**1.** Place the butter, chocolate and golden syrup in a bowl over a pan of gently simmering water. Stir until melted.
**2.** Crush the biscuits by hand or in a bag tied at one end with an elastic band and (carefully) bash with a rolling pin. This is lots of fun!
**3.** Remove the pan from the heat and mix all the ingredients together well.
**4.** Pat the mixture into a baking tray and place in the fridge till set.
**5.** Cut into squares — these scrumptious chocolate slices will go like wild fire!!

## CHOCOLATE VANILLA FUDGE

### INGREDIENTS
100g plain chocolate
50g butter
4 tbsp single cream
1 tsp vanilla essence
450g icing sugar, sifted

### METHOD
**1.** Break the chocolate into pieces and place with the butter into a bowl over a saucepan of hot water. Stir until melted.
**2.** Remove bowl from basin and stir in cream, vanilla essence and sifted icing sugar.
**3.** Spread into a baking tray and chill until set.
**4.** Cut into little squares.

## CHOCOLATE TRUFFLES

### INGREDIENTS
275g milk chocolate
140ml double cream
FOR COATING
Melted chocolate, eg milk or white chocolate
cocoa powder
chopped nuts

### METHOD
**1.** Chop the chocolate finely.
**2.** Heat the cream over a gentle heat until just boiling.
**3.** Remove immediately and stir in the chopped chocolate until smooth.
**4.** Pour into a glass bowl and chill until firm.
**5.** Take a teaspoon of mixture and roll into a ball. Chill again if too soft.
**6.** Coat in melted chocolate, roll in cocoa powder or chopped nuts. Have lots of fun decorating with melted chocolate, chopped nuts and glace fruits.
**7.** Put into pretty paper cases — these truffles make beautiful Christmas presents.

**\*Always ask an adult's permission before using kitchen equipment.**

# Do Not Disturb!

**Meet Stacey,** aged 11, from Lancashire, who's going to show us some of her favourite things.

This is my little brother, Gary, who's a bit of a pest. At least we agree on one thing — we both support Manchester United. My favourite player is David Beckham.

Some of my favourite cuddly toys — and my Spice Girls poster.

This is me on the keyboard. I was given it as a Christmas present.

I help Dad out by typing letters on my word processor.

These are some of my fave dancing outfits.

Me in my modern dance outfit with some of my medals.

This is my collection of Disney characters.

My favourite doll. I don't have a name for her — I just call her "Doll".

STACEY'S ROOM

99

A few days later, there was bad news for Lizzie's family —

BUT THE OLD SQUIRE SAID WE COULD STAY HERE FOR AS LONG AS WE WANTED — SURELY SIR ROBERT WILL NOT TURN US OUT!

I'M SORRY, BUT HE PLANS TO EXPAND THE ESTATE FARM AND ALL THE COTTAGES WILL BE NEEDED FOR THE WORKERS. YOU HAVE A WEEK TO MOVE OUT.

OH, LIZZIE — WHAT ARE WE TO DO? WHERE CAN WE GO?

WE'LL FIND SOMEWHERE. DON'T DESPAIR, MAMA.

THE ONLY THING IS TO GO AND PLEAD WITH SIR ROBERT.

So, Lizzie went to Springwood Hall —

I WANT TO SPEAK TO SIR ROBERT.

WELL, SIR ROBERT WON'T SPEAK TO YOU! BE OFF, GIRL!

But, just then —

WHAT IS WRONG, MY DEAR?

OH! LOOK AT THAT CHILD! I — I CAN'T BELIEVE IT!

SIR ROBERT! LADY ANNE!

WAIT HERE, GIRL.

YES, SIR.

Some time later, Lizzie was taken into the house.

TWO YEARS AGO, WE LOST OUR ONLY CHILD, A DEARLY-BELOVED DAUGHTER. SHE WOULD HAVE BEEN ABOUT YOUR AGE NOW.

YOU ARE SO LIKE HER, MY DEAR! I COULD NOT BELIEVE IT WHEN I SAW YOU FIRST. YOU COULD HAVE BEEN OUR BETH!

OH! I'M SORRY, MA'AM! I DIDN'T MEAN TO UPSET YOU. I AM LIZZIE SMITH. I ONLY CAME TO ASK A GREAT FAVOUR OF SIR ROBERT . . .

101

A MOMENT, MY DEAR! FIRST *WE* HAVE A FAVOUR TO ASK OF *YOU*.

WE KNOW WE CAN NEVER REPLACE OUR BELOVED BETH, BUT TO HAVE A DAUGHTER AGAIN WOULD BE A GREAT JOY TO US. WE ARE ASKING YOU TO COME AND LIVE WITH US, LIZZIE! WE WOULD ADOPT YOU AND YOU WOULD BE TREATED LIKE OUR DAUGHTER.

*WHAT?* BUT I COULDN'T LEAVE MAMA NOW WE HAVE TO GET OUT OF OUR COTTAGE.

IF YOU AGREE TO COME TO US, YOUR FAMILY WILL BE FREE TO STAY IN THEIR COTTAGE.

PLEASE SAY YOU'LL COME TO US, LIZZIE! WE HAVE HEARD WHAT A SWEET GIRL YOU ARE AND WE WILL DO ALL WE CAN TO MAKE YOU HAPPY.

YES, I'LL COME.

HOW CAN I REFUSE? IF I DO, MAMA AND THE FAMILY WILL BE HOMELESS.

EXCELLENT! YOU WILL NOT REGRET YOUR DECISION, MY DEAR!

THE ONLY CONDITION IS THAT YOU MUST NOT TELL ANYONE ABOUT OUR ARRANGEMENT. YOU MAY COLLECT YOUR BELONGINGS, BUT AFTER THAT YOU ARE NOT TO SEE YOUR FAMILY AGAIN. DO YOU UNDERSTAND?

YES, I UNDERSTAND.

FOR MY FAMILY'S SAKE, I MUST AGREE.

Lizzie was driven back in the Springwoods' carriage.

OH, LIZZIE — HOW CAN YOU LEAVE US? YOU WILL NOT BE HAPPY IN THE BIG HOUSE. PLEASE STAY WITH US.

WHAT? STAY HERE WHEN I HAVE THE CHANCE OF LIVING WITH SIR ROBERT AND LADY ANNE? I SHALL HAVE FINE CLOTHES AND SERVANTS TO LOOK AFTER ME.

IF ONLY I COULD EXPLAIN WHY I AM LEAVING. THIS IS HEARTBREAKING!

I CAN'T BEAR TO THINK I MAY NEVER SEE MY DEAR FAMILY AGAIN. BUT AT LEAST I KNOW THEY WILL HAVE A HOME FOR AS LONG AS THEY NEED IT.

In Lizzie's new home —

THIS WAY, *MISS* LIZZIE — ER — ELIZABETH.

I KNOW THE SERVANTS ARE ALL LAUGHING AT ME! EVERYONE KNOWS I AM REALLY PLAIN LIZZIE SMITH.

WHAT A BEAUTIFUL ROOM! AND THOSE DRESSES ARE FOR ME. BUT ALL THE FRILLS AND LACE IN THE WORLD WON'T MAKE ME HAPPY! I'D RATHER BE BACK HOME.

Just then —

SO *YOU'RE* THE COMMON PEASANT UNCLE ROBERT WANTS TO BE HIS DAUGHTER! WELL, SIR ROBERT HAS PROMISED *I* WILL INHERIT THE ESTATE AND DON'T YOU FORGET IT!

CLARISSA, THE SPRINGWOODS' NIECE, I PRESUME.

Later, downstairs —

CLARISSA WILL SHOW YOU AROUND, ELIZABETH. IT HAS BEEN LONELY FOR HER HERE. I KNOW SHE WILL BE PLEASED TO HAVE A COMPANION.

YES, I AM, UNCLE ROBERT. ELIZABETH AND I ARE FRIENDS ALREADY!

HMPH! WE ARE TO BE NOTHING OF THE SORT — CLARISSA HAS MADE THAT PLAIN TO ME. I DON'T THINK SHE WILL MAKE MY LIFE HERE EASY.

At dinner —

NO, ELIZABETH, MY DEAR! THAT'S NOT THE RIGHT KNIFE. YOU MUST USE THE OTHER ONE.

THIS IS DREADFUL! I'M DOING ALL THE WRONG THINGS AND I KNOW CLARISSA AND THE SERVANTS ARE LAUGHING AT ME.

That night —

IF ONLY I WAS BACK IN THE COTTAGE WITH MAMA AND THE OTHERS! LADY ANNE HAS TRIED HER BEST TO PUT ME AT MY EASE, BUT I KNOW I CAN NEVER BE HAPPY HERE.

103

Then —

OW! YOU TRIPPED ME ON PURPOSE, YOU PIG!

ENOUGH OF THIS! GO AND SIT DOWN, MISS ELIZABETH. YOU MAY NOT JOIN IN IF YOU CAN'T BEHAVE YOURSELF.

Later, when Clarissa told Lady Anne what had happened —

OH, ELIZABETH! I'M DISAPPOINTED IN YOU! YOU MUST WRITE A LETTER OF APOLOGY AT ONCE.

I'M SORRY.

YOU *ARE* HAPPY WITH US, AREN'T YOU? I KNOW IT'S DIFFICULT FOR YOU TO LEARN NEW WAYS, BUT IT MEANS SO MUCH TO ROBERT AND ME.

YES — ER — OF COURSE I'M HAPPPY HERE. YOU ARE BOTH SO KIND TO ME.

The weeks passed and soon it was Christmas —

DID YOU KNOW YOUR MOTHER'S VERY POORLY, MISS ELIZABETH? I DON'T SUPPOSE IT MATTERS TO YOU, LIVING HERE IN THE BIG HOUSE.

THE SERVANTS ALL THINK I CHOSE TO ABANDON MY FAMILY TO COME AND LIVE HERE. POOR MAMA! IF ONLY I COULD GO TO SEE HER.

I'LL SEND THESE GOLD SOVEREIGNS THAT SIR ROBERT GAVE ME TO MAMA. THAT SHOULD BUY FOOD AND MEDICINE AND PRESENTS FOR THE FAMILY.

Lizzie sent her gift with one of the servants, but later —

MAMA WOULDN'T TAKE A GIFT FROM ME! SHE'S SENT THE MONEY BACK. HOW SHE MUST HATE ME!

105

# Great Grandma's Sweet Shop Secrets

1 Bunty reader, Amy Shepherd, visited Beamish Open Air Museum and gazed longingly into the window of the Victorian Jubilee Confectioners.

2 The Jubilee Sweet Shop is set in the town area of Beamish where tram cars criss-cross along the street dropping off customers.

3 Amy's taste buds could stand it no longer. She just had to sample the wares inside the shop!

4 In the back shop, John the sweet maker was busy bubbling up another batch of yummy sweets.

**5** Amy watched as John placed the mixture into the punching mangle and out of the other end came shiny black marble balls.

**6** Amy had great fun separating them! What a lovely crunching sound!

**7** Back in the front shop, Amy, watched by the other assistants, wrapped up the sweets for the next customer.

●This is how Amy would have looked in her great-great grandmother's day as an assistant in the Jubilee Confectioners shop.

**8** Then it was into costume to do her stint behind the counter.

# Pretend Friends

HI! MY NAME'S STACEY BARRATT. A FEW MONTHS AGO, MY MATES WERE GIVING ME REAL BOTHER.

DAVID'S NICE! WHY DON'T YOU GO OUT WITH HIM?

OR MURRAY. HE'S BEEN ON HIS OWN SINCE ALISON CHUCKED HIM.

NO! LOOK, I'VE TOLD YOU! I DON'T WANT A BOYFRIEND!

BUT WE'VE ALL GOT ONE!

YEAH! YOU'RE MISSING OUT! IF YOU HAD A BOYFRIEND YOU COULD JOIN IN WHEN WE'RE TALKING ABOUT BOYS.

OH, I GIVE UP! YOU'RE ALL BOY MAD!

HI, STACEY! ON YOUR OWN?

OH, NO! IT'S ROBIN FLETCHER FROM OUR CLASS. I HOPE HE'S NOT PLANNING TO ASK ME OUT.

111

"I decided to make my position quite clear —"

YEAH. I GOT FED UP WITH MY MATES. THEY KEEP TRYING TO PAIR ME OFF, BUT I DON'T WANT TO GO OUT WITH ANYONE.

I KNOW THE FEELING! MY MATES KEEP ON AT ME TO GET A GIRLFRIEND.

OH! SO YOU'VE GOT THE SAME PROBLEM AS ME.

LOOKS LIKE IT. HEY — MAYBE WE COULD DO EACH OTHER A FAVOUR!

HOW DO YOU MEAN?

WE COULD *PRETEND* WE'RE GOING OUT — TO KEEP OUR FRIENDS HAPPY. THAT WOULD STOP THEM TRYING TO PAIR US OFF WITH ANYONE ELSE.

THAT'S A *GREAT* IDEA!

"So, next morning —"

MURRAY'S *DEFINITELY* LOOKING FOR A NEW GIRLFRIEND, KEITH SAID.

REALLY? WELL, IT'S NO GOOD HIM LOOKING AT ME. I'M SPOKEN FOR.

*YOU!* BUT YOU'RE NOT GOING OUT WITH ANYONE.

I AM *NOW!* ROBIN FLETCHER ASKED ME OUT AFTER I'D LEFT YOU LAST NIGHT.

112

HERE HE COMES NOW. HI, ROBIN!

HI, STACEY! HOW'S MY GIRLFRIEND THIS MORNING?

SO YOU TWO *ARE* GOING OUT!

AMAZING!

LOOK AT THEIR FACES! THIS WAS A BRILL IDEA!

"The following week —"

I'M HAVING A PARTY ON SATURDAY. YOU AND ROBIN MUST COME.

GREAT! THANKS!

IS THAT OKAY, ROBIN?

SURE! MY MATES HAVE BEEN INVITED, TOO. THEY'LL EXPECT TO SEE US THERE TOGETHER.

"It was a great party."

I'M HAVING A LOVELY TIME.

ME, TOO. AND WE WOULDN'T HAVE BEEN INVITED IF MARIE HADN'T THOUGHT WE WERE GOING OUT TOGETHER. IT'S STRICTLY COUPLES.

"Not that we spent all evening together —"

YOU HAVEN'T DANCED WITH ROBIN FOR AGES, STACEY.

OH, THAT'S OKAY. WE HAVE A VERY OPEN RELATIONSHIP.

113

WHAT A LAUGH! WE'VE GOT ALL OUR FRIENDS FOOLED!

YES. THIS WAS A BRILLIANT IDEA OF YOURS, ROBIN!

"Then, one day —"

WHERE'S YOUR BOYFRIEND TODAY, STACEY?

OH—I—ER DON'T KNOW.

MESSAGE FOR YOU, STACEY. ROBIN'S GOT A COLD.

OH — OKAY. THANKS, MIKE.

WHAT A SHAME! YOU WON'T BE ABLE TO SEE HIM FOR A FEW DAYS.

THAT DOESN'T BOTHER ME. HE'S NOT MY *REAL* BOYFRIEND, SO I DON'T MIND.

"But, to my surprise, I found I *DID* mind."

JANICE SAYS THERE'S A GREAT NEW MAKE-UP STALL IN THE MARKET.

I WONDER WHAT ROBIN'S DOING NOW?

WHAT DO YOU THINK, STACEY? SHALL WE GO THERE?

EH? *WHERE?*

SHE'S NOT LISTENING. SHE'S OBVIOUSLY PINING FOR ROBIN.

I THINK SHE'S RIGHT! I *DO* MISS HIM!

"During Maths, I made a decision."

I KNOW I SAID I DIDN'T WANT A BOYFRIEND, BUT I WAS WRONG.

ARE YOU COMING TO THE MARKET WITH US NOW?

NO. I'M GOING TO VISIT ROBIN.

I CAN'T WAIT TO SEE HIM AGAIN.

"But —"

MAYBE HE'S CHANGED HIS MIND ABOUT ME, TOO. I HOPE SO.

IT WAS A GREAT IDEA YOU COMING TO SEE ME. KEEPING UP THE PRETENCE, EH?

ER . . .YEAH.

IT'S SUCH A LAUGH, ISN'T IT, STACEY?

I'VE GOT A PRETEND BOYFRIEND — BUT I WANT HIM TO BE MY *REAL* ONE.

"Then, suddenly, Robin's kid brother came barging in —"

MUM SAYS DOES YOUR FRIEND WANT A COFFEE?

NO, THANKS. I'M JUST LEAVING.

IS THIS STACEY?

THAT'S RIGHT.

HE FANCIES YOU! HE WROTE IT IN HIS DIARY. I PEEKED!

YOU LITTLE SNEAK! GET OUT!

SORRY ABOUT HIM I . . . ER . . . HAD TO WRITE I FANCIED YOU TO KEEP UP THE PRETENCE.

IN YOUR *DIARY*? SURELY YOUR MATES DON'T READ *THAT*?

WELL . . . NO. OH, I MIGHT AS WELL ADMIT IT. SINCE WE'VE BEEN PRETENDING TO GO OUT, I'VE ACTUALLY FALLEN FOR YOU. I KNOW IT'S POINTLESS, THOUGH. YOU DON'T WANT A BOYFRIEND.

BUT I *DO*! I WANT *YOU*!

THIS IS GREAT, STACEY! SO YOU *WILL* GO OUT WITH ME?

YOU BET!

AND, THIS TIME, IT'S FOR REAL!

*The End*

# NO CHRISTMAS FOR CAROL

A SHORT time before Christmas, Carol and her friend Holly were out shopping.

CAN I HELP YOU? I BET YOU'RE BOTH LOOKING FORWARD TO CHRISTMAS.

NOT LIKELY — WE *HATE* CHRISTMAS!

IMAGINE ACTUALLY BEING CALLED CAROL SINGER. I HAVE TO PUT UP WITH SUCH AWFUL JOKES, ESPECIALLY AT THIS TIME OF YEAR.

IT'S NO JOKE BEING BORN ON CHRISTMAS EVE EITHER — OR BEING CALLED HOLLY.

IF ONLY I DIDN'T HAVE TO TAKE PART IN MY STUPID FAMILY SING-ALONG. I CAN'T SING A NOTE!

LET'S GET OUT OF HERE — SOMEWHERE AS FAR AWAY FROM THIS CHRISTMAS NONSENSE AS POSSIBLE.

RIGHT! C'MON.

IT'S AWFUL BEING BORN ON CHRISTMAS EVE. I NEVER GET PROPER BIRTHDAY PRESENTS.

I KNOW WHAT YOU MEAN. CHRISTMAS LEAVES ME COLD, TOO.

118

Later, at Carol's —

SOON HAVE THIS BABY IN THE FRONT ROOM, READY FOR THE FAMILY CONCERT.

CAROL'S BEEN PRACTISING 'SILENT NIGHT'.

OH, NO, SHE HASN'T!

WE SO LOOK FORWARD TO OUR ANNUAL SING-ALONG. IT DOESN'T MATTER THAT WE'RE NOT SUCH GREAT SINGERS, WE ALL HAVE A GOOD TIME.

CAROL DOESN'T. SHE SAYS SHE'S EMBARRASSED BECAUSE SHE'S A ROTTEN SINGER.

OOPS — NOW I'VE DONE IT.

Next day, at school —

SO, WHAT'S SANTA BRINGING YOU, THEN, HOLLY?

SOME PEACE FROM YOU, I HOPE, NATALIE.

IT'S HARD TO CANCEL CHRISTMAS WHEN EVERYONE TALKS ABOUT IT ALL THE TIME.

After school —

LISTEN TO THAT TAPED MUSIC! I'M SICK OF CHRISTMAS CAROLS — PRESENT COMPANY EXCEPTED.

CHARITY CHRISTMAS CARDS

AND ALL THOSE 'YULETIDE' POP SONGS. YEUK!

At home, Carol flicked through the TV channels.

AW, MUM — THERE'S NOTHING ON BUT CHRISTMAS SPECIALS AND ADVERTS FOR LAST MINUTE GIFTS.

119

Even on the school outing —

I DON'T BELIEVE IT! THE SCHOOL OUTING'S TO THE CHRISTMAS PANTOMIME. WHAT A DRAG!

NEVER MIND. IT'S CHRISTMAS EVE TOMORROW. IT'LL SOON BE ALL OVER.

And, on Christmas Eve —

WHAT'S GOING ON? WHERE ARE WE GOING? WHAT ABOUT THE SING-ALONG?

OH, WE'LL BE ABLE TO SING WHERE WE'RE GOING, DON'T YOU WORRY.

In a local hall —

SURPRISE, SURPRISE!

GO ON, HOLLY. BLOW OUT YOUR CANDLES AND MAKE A WISH.

GOSH, A REAL BIRTHDAY PARTY! I THINK MY WISH CAME TRUE ALREADY.

HAPPY BIRTHDAY, DEAR HOLLY, HAPPY BIRTHDAY TO YOU.

WELL, FOR ONE NIGHT ANYWAY, WE CAN FORGET ALL ABOUT CHRISTMAS. THEN, TOMORROW, PERHAPS WE CAN ACTUALLY ENJOY IT FOR ONCE!

THE END

# The FOUR MARYS

THE FOUR MARYS — Mary Cotter, Mary Field, Mary Radleigh and Mary Simpson — were best friends at St Elmo's. Christmas was approaching and the school was involved in all sorts of seasonal activities.

♪ . . . SO PLEASE PUT A PENNY IN THE OLD MAN'S HAT . . . IF YOU HAVEN'T GOT A PENNY, A HA'PENNY WILL DO . . . ♪

Next day, the girls were given a free afternoon to do their shopping.

WE WERE THINKING OF GETTING YOU A FRENCH PHRASE BOOK, COTTY.

HUH?

YEAH, SINCE YOU'RE SURE TO WIN THE DESIGN-A-CHRISTMAS CARD CONTEST WE'RE HAVING AT SCHOOL, WITH ITS FABBY TRIP TO DISNEYLAND PARIS PRIZE.

FOREIGN LANGUAGE DICTIONARIES

WHO SAYS?

EVERYONE. YOU'RE TERRIFIC AT ART.

HI, CAROL.

YOU'RE GOOD AT ART, TOO, CAROL. YOU MIGHT WIN.

THE PARIS THING? I'D LOVE TO. I'VE NEVER BEEN ABROAD.

CAROL'S REALLY NICE, ISN'T SHE?

YES, BUT I HEARD THAT HER FAMILY HAS HIT HARD TIMES AND THEY'RE STRUGGLING TO KEEP HER AT ST ELMO'S.

BARGAIN CORNER HALF PRICE BOOKS

SHAME. I MEAN, THERE'S MABEL AND VERONICA THERE, ROLLING IN IT, AND THEY'RE *SO* AWFUL!

Later —

COME ON, TIM.

I'D LIKE THIS FOR MY MUM BUT I DON'T THINK I'VE GOT ENOUGH. UNLESS . . . I USE MY BUS FARE AND WALK HOME.

123

THE STANDARD'S HIGH, AS MRS MITCHELL SAID. COTTY'S IS BEST, THOUGH.

YEAH, I RECKON IT'S THE CLEAR WINNER.

THAT'S CAROL'S. I'VE HEARD SOME OF THE OTHERS ADMIRING IT TOO — BUT NOT AS MUCH AS COTTY'S, OF COURSE.

IT IS GOOD. BUT IT COULD BE BETTER. THERE'S SOMETHING JUST NOT QUITE RIGHT . . .

YES, WE ALL AGREE — IT'S YOU WHO'LL BE GOING TO PARIS, COTTY. SAY 'HI' TO MICKEY FOR US!

LEAVE IT — I HAVEN'T WON YET.

AND I DON'T WANT TO. I WANT CAROL TO WIN.

I GET TRIPS AWAY ANYWAY, BUT I IMAGINE THE PRIZE IS HER ONLY CHANCE. WISH SHE'D SHOWN ME HER ENTRY BEFORE, BECAUSE I THINK I SEE HOW TO IMPROVE IT. BUT IT'S TOO LATE NOW . . .

Late that night —

YEAH, THAT MAKES ALL THE DIFFERENCE TO THAT . . . SO NOW TO ALTER THIS ONE A BIT TOO . . .

. . . OR IS IT?

124

Next day —

YOU KNOW, SOMEHOW YOUR PICTURE LOOKS *DULLER* TODAY, COTTY.

YEAH, I THOUGHT THERE WAS MORE PINK IN THE SKY, TOO.

OH, IT'S AMAZING HOW DIFFERENT A PICTURE CAN LOOK DEPENDING ON THE LIGHT.

I MEAN, I RECKON CAROL'S LOOK *BETTER* TODAY, TOO, DON'T YOU?

IT DOES. THE CHILD'S FACE IS GLOWING.

And —

. . . SO THE WINNER IS — CAROL BRENT!

I CAN'T ACCEPT IT. MY PICTURE'S CHANGED. I KNOW IT CAN'T HAVE, BUT IT HAS —

MAYBE IT'S LIKE THAT BOY DROPPING THE MONEY, CAROL . . .

. . . ANYTHING CAN HAPPEN AT CHRISTMAS. TAKE THE PRIZE.

Later —

I DON'T KNOW. YOU *SAY* IT'S JUST THE LIGHT, COTTY, BUT I'M NOT SURE —

YEAH, I THINK THERE'S SOMETHING ELSE TOO!

THE OTHERS WILL NEVER KNOW I CHANGED THE PICTURES. I'M JUST GLAD CAROL'S WON AND WILL HAVE A MERRY CHRISTMAS.

**The End**

# ...And A Hap

We asked the West Jesmond Junior School Netball team to tell us their New Year Resolutions.

**Sarah Kinghorn (12)**
Try to be nice to my 8-year-old brother, even when he's annoying and goes into my room and mixes up all my stuff, and nicks my pens and pencils. I shout at him and I RESOLVE not to shout at him any more!
Not to eat pork, lamb or beef.
Not to talk in class — only when the teacher says.
Not to bite my nails.

**Nicola Singh (12)**
To ride my horse Thingyimly more often, and to stop myself sleep walking because last time I walked to school and let all the frogs free in the science lab . . . and to watch more "X Files"!!!

**Sarah Mattok (12)**
To stop hiccuping as my brother hates it!
To brush and groom the cat at least once a week.

**Sophie Hilton (12)**
To help keep the environment clean and tidy. I like trees and want to see them preserved, but I'm not quite sure how.
To stop annoying my brother (difficult one, huh!!).

**Anna Thagesen (12)**
Not to talk as much in class, and be nice to everyone.
I am also resolving to keep in touch with all my mates in England when I move back to Denmark.

**Vicky Miller (12)**
Not to bite my nails (but I say that every year!).
To brush my dog more often, and to hold my guinea pigs more.
I resolve to win a fortune this year and make life more exciting for my friends.

**Jo-anne McClafferty (12)**
To make time for more netball practice.
To clean my teeth much more — then I won't have to go to the dentist!
Not to bite my nails, but to paint them pink, blue, orange, purple and green!